creatures
of the sea

Creatures That Glow

Other titles in the series:
Beluga Whales
Coral
The Crab
Dolphins
Flying Fish
Humpback Whales
Jellyfish
Lobsters
Moray Eels
The Octopus
Rays
Sea Horses
Sea Stars
Squid
The Walrus
The Whale Shark

creatures of the sea

Creatures That Glow

Kris Hirschmann

KIDHAVEN PRESS
An imprint of Thomson Gale, a part of The Thomson Corporation

Detroit • New York • San Francisco • San Diego • New Haven, Conn.
Waterville, Maine • London • Munich

St. Mary's Episcopal School
Kelsey Zehring Library
41 N. Perkins
Memphis, TN 38117

© 2005 Thomson Gale, a part of The Thomson Corporation.

Thomson and Star Logo are trademarks and Gale and Kidhaven Press are registered trademarks used herein under license.

For more information, contact
KidHaven Press
27500 Drake Rd.
Farmington Hills, MI 48331-3535
Or you can visit our Internet site at http://www.gale.com

ALL RIGHTS RESERVED.
No part of this work covered by the copyright hereon may be reproduced or used in any form or by any means—graphic, electronic, or mechanical, including photocopying, recording, taping, Web distribution or information storage retrieval systems—without the written permission of the publisher.

LIBRARY OF CONGRESS CATALOGING-IN-PUBLICATION DATA

Hirschmann, Kris, 1967–
 Creatures that glow / by Kris Hirschmann.
  p. cm. — (Creatures of the sea)
 Includes bibliographical references (p. 43).
 ISBN 0-7377-2340-8 (hardcover : alk. paper)
 1. Bioluminescence—Juvenile literature. 2. Marine animals—Juvenile literature. 3. Marine plants—Juvenile literature. I. Title.
 QH641.H558 2005
 572'.4358—dc22
                                                         2004020951

Printed in the United States of America

Table of Contents

Introduction
Who Glows There?   6

Chapter 1
Oceans Aglow   9

Chapter 2
Communication and Reproduction   17

Chapter 3
On the Hunt   25

Chapter 4
Staying Alive   33

Glossary   41

For Further Exploration   43

Index   45

Picture Credits   47

About the Author   48

Introduction

Who Glows There?

Anyone who has ever swum in the ocean can picture the gentle, shifting light that fills the water during the daytime hours. This light, however, is a fleeting thing. At night, with no sun sending its rays toward the water, the upper regions of the sea go dark. And sunlight never travels below the very shallowest parts of the sea. Even on the brightest days, the midlevel and deep parts of the ocean remain cold and sunless.

But when sunlight fades, an amazing thing happens. The seas light up with millions upon millions of blue-green dots. These tiny lanterns swirl like snowflakes through every part of the ocean, from the extreme upper regions to the deepest, darkest depths. In some places the lights swarm so thickly

Who Glows There? **7**

Most sea creatures can produce their own light. Here, coral polyps glow while feeding at night.

that the water itself glows. This glow is the telltale sign of **bioluminescence**, living light that is created within a creature's body.

On land, bioluminescence is a rare thing. It is found mostly in fireflies, some species of worms, and a few types of fungus. In the ocean, however, bioluminescence is extremely common. Scientists estimate that more than 80 percent of the sea's creatures are able to produce their own glow. In the upper regions of the ocean, the percentage may be even higher. It is believed that up to 90 percent of the animals that live in shallow regions can make light within their bodies.

It makes sense that bioluminescence is so common in the earth's seas. Nearly three-quarters of the planet's surface is covered by water, and most of this water is deep and dark. By giving ocean creatures the ability to glow, nature makes vision possible at all depths and in all circumstances. And in the sea, as on land, vision is an important sense that can help an animal do many things, including communicate, reproduce, hunt, and protect itself. So bioluminescence is not just lovely; it is also a survival tool. In the harsh ocean world, creatures that glow may just be creatures that stay alive as well.

Oceans Aglow

Bioluminescence is defined as light created by an **organism** through a chemical reaction. Unlike most light, bioluminescence creates no heat. A person can safely hold any glowing creature in his or her hand without getting burned.

Most ocean residents are bioluminescent. Glowing sea creatures include small organisms such as bacteria, algae, shrimp, worms, and krill. Larger animals, such as jellyfish, squid, sea stars, sharks, and fish, may also glow. In some families, such as the jellyfish and the squid, nearly all species are bioluminescent. In other families, such as the clams and octopuses, just a few species have this ability.

Follow the Glow

Bioluminescent animals can be seen in every ocean in the world, from the warm tropical waters near the equator to the icy regions near the north and south poles. They also live in all of the earth's seas and even in some lagoons that contain salty or brackish (partly salty) water. Within the seas, bioluminescence is found at all levels, from the shallowest to the deepest waters. This phenomenon is most easily seen in deep parts of the sea where sunlight cannot penetrate. With no light to mask their glow, millions of tiny creatures fill the inky waters with a blizzard of sparkles.

However, it is not necessary to travel far below the ocean's surface to see bioluminescence. In some parts of the world, in fact, it is not even necessary to enter the water. Glowing bacteria or one-celled organisms called **dinoflagellates** may gather in such huge numbers that the water shines with a gentle blue green hue. One of the most famous viewing spots for this phenomenon is Puerto Rico's Mosquito Bay. This lagoon, which is attached by a narrow channel to the Caribbean Sea, glows green every night of the year. The wakes of boats passing through the bay light up as millions of dinoflagellates flash, and people who enter the water can make glowing trails by waving their arms and legs back and forth.

Less predictable but even more spectacular are the rare bioluminescent displays that happen in the

When large numbers of these bacteria known as dinoflagellates glow (inset), the water lights up with a bluish green color.

Indian Ocean and the Arabian Sea. When conditions are just right, miles of water may shine softly from the light of millions of tiny bioluminescent creatures. Sailors call these displays "milky seas" because of the soft white glow these creatures produce.

Bioluminescence can often be seen even in areas not particularly known for this phenomenon. Waves breaking against shores around the world may be outlined in a rich blue glow. Fishermen sometimes find their nets drenched with shining water when they are pulled up from the deep. And on ships, where seawater is used in toilets, a greenish glow can often be seen if the bathroom light is turned off.

Flushing disturbs the water in the toilet, causing the tiny creatures that swim in the water to flash their living lights.

How It Works

All bioluminescence is produced by chemical reactions. Two substances are needed to create these reactions. One is a **protein** known as a **luciferin**, and the other is an **enzyme** known as a **luciferase**. When these two substances come together in the presence of oxygen, a chemical reaction occurs that joins the luciferin and the oxygen into a new chemical called an **oxyluciferin**. At the same time, energy is produced. This energy is released in the form of light.

Once formed, oxyluciferins are inactive, which means they cannot participate in chemical reactions. And the original luciferin cannot break free of the oxygen. In terms of bioluminescence, it is now useless. So most bioluminescent creatures must constantly rebuild their luciferin supplies. Many animals get fresh luciferin directly from the foods they eat. Others can build luciferin within their bodies from a combination of raw materials. One way or another, a creature can usually gather everything it needs to keep itself glowing strong.

The words *luciferin* and *luciferase* do not actually refer to specific chemicals. They are general terms for many different proteins and enzymes that perform the same job in different creatures.

Oceans Aglow

How Bioluminescence Works

Light is produced when a protein called a luciferin and an enzyme called a luciferase combine in the presence of oxygen.

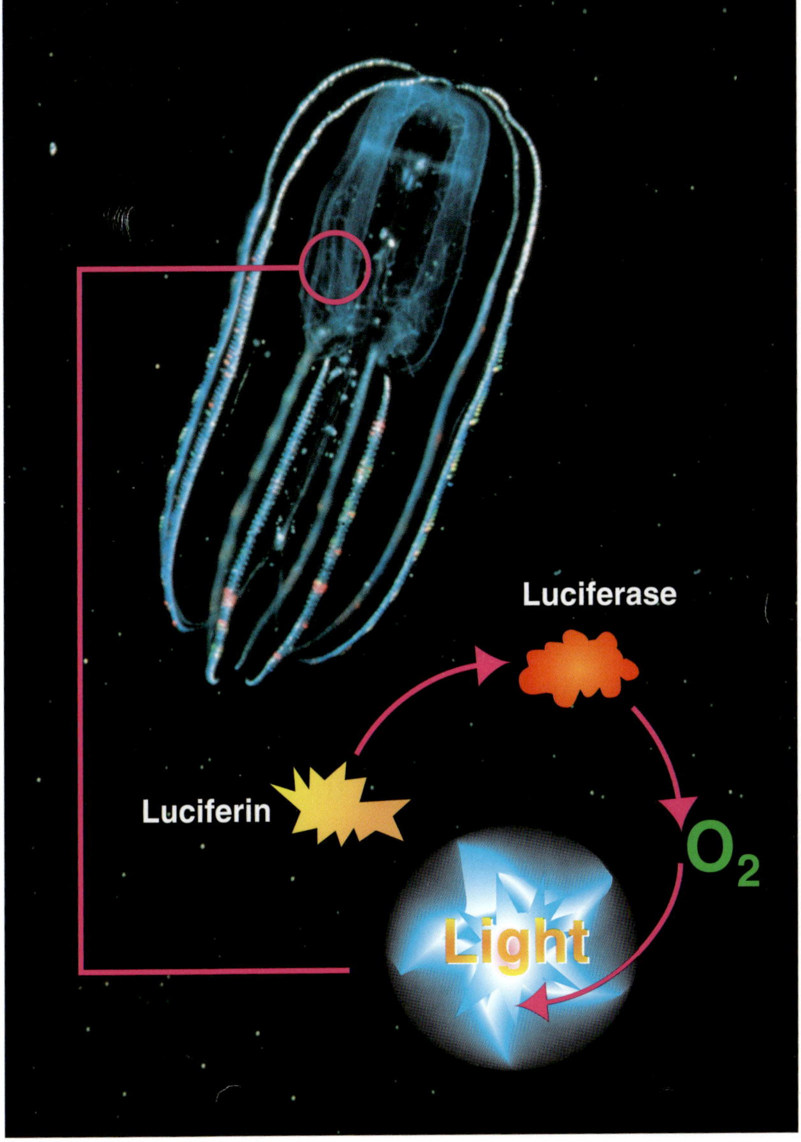

Luciferase

Luciferin

O_2

Light

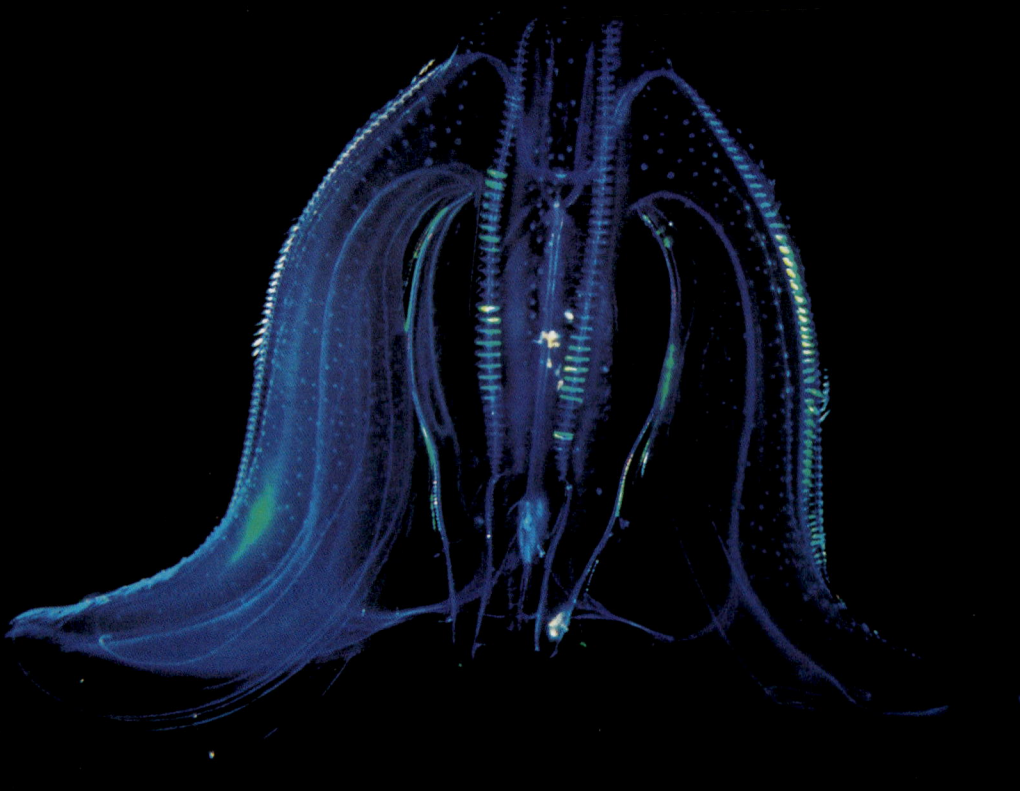

This comb jelly glows blue, the most common color for bioluminescence.

Depending on the exact chemicals involved, the glow from a reaction may look very different. Differences in color are especially common. Bioluminescence can be any color in the rainbow, including green, red, orange, yellow, and violet. Jellyfish in particular are known for their spectacular color displays, sometimes flashing multiple hues when they are disturbed. At least one type of squid glows green, and some fish produce deep red lights. By far the most common color for bioluminescence, however, is blue.

Types of Bioluminescence

There are three types of bioluminescence. The simplest type is produced outside an animal's body by a chemical reaction in the water. Creatures that make this type of bioluminescence have separate sacs inside their bodies for luciferins and luciferases. When they want to make light, the creatures squirt these substances out of their bodies. The luciferins and luciferases come together with seawater and oxygen, causing a sudden burst of brightness. Some squids use this process to make clouds of glowing ink. Certain mussels also have separate luciferin and luciferase sacs within their bodies. If they are crushed and mixed with water, these mussels will continue to glow long after they have died.

A second type of bioluminescence is created inside a creature's body. This type of bioluminescence is sometimes called **intracellular bioluminescence** because the luciferin and luciferase react within an organism's cells. Bacteria, algae, and other microscopic creatures use this method to set their entire bodies aglow. In larger animals, such as fish and squid, light-producing cells may be arranged into special organs called **photophores.** Photophores are like built-in flashlights that a creature can turn on and off at will by starting and stopping chemical reactions inside the body. Depending on the species, photophores may contain reflectors that can point light in a specific direction, spread it out, or even change its color and intensity.

The last type of bioluminescence is called **bacterial bioluminescence**. Creatures that use this

Creatures That Glow

Some creatures store colonies of bioluminescent bacteria like these in their bodies to help them glow.

method take glowing bacteria into their bodies. Then they store the bacteria inside special sacs with see-through coverings. Flashlight fish, for example, keep colonies of bioluminescent bacteria in kidney-shaped pouches under their eyes. The sacs give off a bright light that lets the fish see in dark conditions. Anglerfish, too, use bacteria to help them glow. These fish dangle shining pouches of bacteria in front of their toothy mouths to attract prey.

An Important Ability

The fact that there are so many types of bioluminescence—and so many different chemical reactions that produce it—suggests that the ability to glow has evolved over and over again in the ocean world. This has happened because bioluminescence is such a useful tool. In nature, traits that help animals survive get passed on to future generations. This has certainly been true of bioluminescence, which is the main source of light in the ocean realm.

chapter

2

Communication and Reproduction

In the sea, as on land, most creatures must communicate with each other to survive. Bioluminescence is often used for this purpose. By flashing its living lights, an animal can broadcast its location. It can also use special light arrangements or blinking rhythms to send messages about its wants and needs, such as finding a mate.

Most creatures that communicate with bioluminescence keep their displays to a minimum. Blinking lights may attract **predators**, so they are used only when necessary. But even an occasional burst of light can be very useful in the deep, dark depths of the ocean.

Creatures That Glow

Talking with Light

One creature that is well known for communicating with light is the flashlight fish, which has brightly lit pouches under its eyes. Found mostly in the Pacific and Indian oceans, these small animals are the brightest creatures on earth. The glow of a single flashlight fish can be seen from as much as 100 feet (30m) away, and groups of flashlight fish are visible from an even greater distance. Together, these animals sometimes look like bright spotlights moving far below the water's surface. During wartime, schools of flashlight fish have been shot at because soldiers thought they were enemy divers carrying searchlights.

A bioluminescent jellyfish glows a dark red color in order to scare off potential predators.

Flashlight fish communicate by using brilliantly lit pouches found beneath their eyes.

Humans are not the only creatures that can see the glow of the flashlight fish. Other flashlight fish also see the lights shining from their relatives' faces. They use these lights to find each other and to form schools when conditions are dark. They may also signal to each other by turning their lights on and off. Depending on the species, a flashlight fish does this either by drawing dark flaps of skin over its bioluminescent pouches or by rotating the pouches backward into its head.

Shrimplike creatures called krill also use bioluminescence as a schooling aid. There are more than eighty different species of krill, and nearly all of them have the ability to glow. These small animals gather in enormous schools that may contain millions of individuals. They flash bluish lights along the bottoms

20 Creatures That Glow

This deep-sea octopus has glowing suckers on its tentacles that send signals to other octopuses.

of their bodies to signal to their schoolmates and keep their groups together.

Octopuses do not school, but it seems that at least one species does use bioluminescence for communication. Scientists have discovered a deep-sea octopus whose arms are lined with rows of glowing suckers. Shallow-water octopuses display their suckers as a way of sending signals to other octopuses, so it is likely that this deepwater species is doing the same thing. In a world without light, the suckers must shine to be seen.

Communication and Reproduction

Finding a Mate

All creatures must reproduce to keep their species alive. Before they can reproduce, however, most animals need to find mates. In the dark ocean, many creatures use bioluminescence to do just that.

Crustaceans called **ostracods** are one type of animal that uses bioluminescence to attract mates. These tiny creatures measure only about 1/30 of an inch (less than 1mm) from end to end. When it is time to mate, male ostracods swim just above the

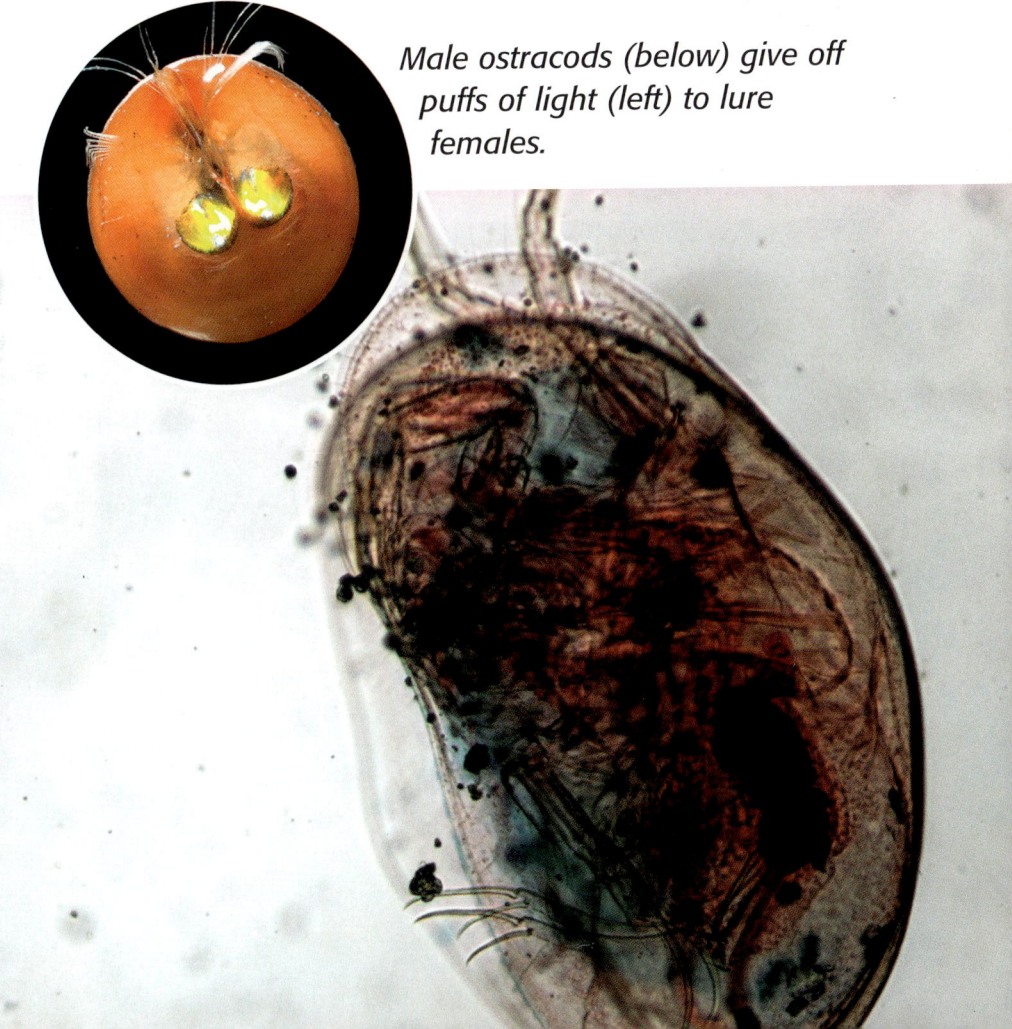

Male ostracods (below) give off puffs of light (left) to lure females.

seafloor giving off little puffs of light. Females living on the bottom recognize males of the correct species mostly by their swimming direction and the rate of their light puffs. The kind of terrain over which the display occurs (for example, sandy bottom vs. coral reef) and the time of day and year are other important clues. When the signals are just right, females leave the ocean floor and join the males to spawn. The water comes alive with sparkles as more and more ostracods begin their mating dance.

Some creatures use light patterns on their bodies to catch the attention of possible spawning partners. Certain squid, for example, may flash their lights as a

Female anglerfish use the bioluminescent organ on top of their head to attract mating partners.

Communication and Reproduction

mating signal. In other species, females have one type of light organ and males have another. Deep-sea lantern fish and hatchetfish, for example, have distinct arrangements of light organs on their bodies that clearly identify their species. Scientists believe that these species use their glow to tell members of the opposite sex that they are ready to mate.

Creatures called anglerfish take the light-recognition technique to the extreme. These fish live in the deepest parts of the ocean, where sunlight never penetrates. In this inky black environment, male anglerfish recognize females by the shape of a lighted organ dangling from the head. The male, which does not have any light organs, swims over to the much larger female and bites into her side. Before long the male's lips actually become part of the female's flesh. Attached for life, neither of the fish will ever have to look for another mate. The male anglerfish is right there to provide sperm whenever the female wants to lay eggs. This mating technique is very practical for anglerfish, which are solitary creatures that may have trouble finding each other when spawning season arrives.

Mating Displays

Some creatures put on incredible light displays during the mating process. One of the best-known examples of this phenomenon comes from the Bermuda fireworm. As its name suggests, this animal is common in the waters around Bermuda, but it can also be found in many other parts of the world. Fire worms live on the seafloor most of the time. But several days after a full moon, female fire worms take to the water about fifty minutes after sunset. They spiral to the surface, releasing glowing strings of eggs as they swim. Male fire worms soon follow the females. They swim into the center of the glowing egg mass and flash their bodies on and off as they release sperm. The entire process takes just a few minutes. Then the fire worms go dark and sink back to the ocean floor, where they will remain until the following month.

Another remarkable mating display happens in Japan's Toyama Bay from March through May. At this time firefly squid, which usually live deep below the sea surface, migrate to shallow waters to breed. Bearing more than one thousand lights on their bodies, heads, and tentacles, these creatures brighten the water with blue flashes as they spawn. Thousands of tourists travel to Toyama Bay each year to see this incredible natural fireworks show.

It is likely that many other creatures use bioluminescence during the mating process. Because many of the world's glowing animals live deep in the sea, however, scientists do not know much about how or when their lights are used. As technology continues to advance, perhaps researchers will learn more about these fascinating deepwater residents.

chapter 3

On the Hunt

In the ocean world, the search for food is a never-ending task that takes up most of an animal's time. To make this task easier, every creature has developed its own special ways of finding things to eat. Some animals depend on traits such as sharp teeth or powerful bodies. For other animals, the ability to glow has become an essential hunting tool. Bioluminescence helps hungry creatures see in the dark, coordinate attacks, and attract prey. Without this feature, many of the ocean's animals would not be able to survive.

Looking for Food

All levels of the ocean contain active predators, or creatures that move around and look for food. Bioluminescence can be a huge help to these animals,

26 Creatures That Glow

Female anglerfish dangle their bioluminescent organ like glowing bait to lure prey into their mouths.

On the Hunt

Some bioluminescent fish have photophores on the sides of their bodies to signal and attract prey.

especially those that live in sunless regions. The dwarf lantern shark of Colombia is a good example. These deepwater dwellers have distinctive patterns of photophores on their bodies. Scientists think that these patterns help dwarf lantern sharks to coordinate attacks on squid. Without bioluminescence, hunting groups might have a hard time staying together in the dark.

Some types of cardinal fish use a similar technique when looking for food. These small fish are found in shallow water. During the daytime, they hide in underwater caves and cracks. At night, they come out to look for tiny crustaceans and other **zooplankton** (microscopic floating animals). They swim in groups over coral reefs, shining their living lights as they go. Photophore patterns on the cardinal fish's sides help group members to see and follow each other as long as the hunt continues.

Some sea creatures use their lights not just to keep track of each other but also as searchlights. Flashlight fish are especially well known for this behavior. Just by pointing its head in a certain direction, a flashlight fish can brighten an area to look for prey. Once a tasty animal is found, the flashlight fish starts glowing even brighter. The extra light helps the flashlight fish to see while it chases down and swallows its prey.

Seeing in the Dark

One of the ocean's most unusual hunting techniques is used by a deepwater creature called the black dragonfish. Like the flashlight fish, black dragonfish have bioluminescent pouches beneath their eyes. Instead of shining blue or blue-green like the light organs of most creatures, however, these pouches give off a deep red light. Most deep-sea creatures do not have **receptors** in their eyes for red light; they literally cannot see it. But black dragonfish can. They use their red glow to brighten the area just in front of their bodies and spot any prey that may be swimming past.

This species of dragonfish, called a black belly dragonfish, has a bioluminescent organ that juts straight out from its chin.

The prey does not notice the black dragonfish's light, so it does not try to escape. Before it knows what is happening, the unlucky animal has been snapped up by the hungry predator.

The black dragonfish's light does not start out red. When the light is first created inside the fish's photophores, it is a typical blue-green color. Special **pigments** inside the photophores absorb the light and send it back out again as red light. This red light then passes through a filtering lens that deepens the color. By the time the light leaves the black dragonfish's body, it is so dark that it is nearly **infrared** (a red so deep that it cannot be seen by the human eye). This incredible adaptation is unique in nature.

Creatures That Glow

It gives the black dragonfish a huge advantage in its pitch-black home, where bioluminescence can act as a blazing warning to potential meals.

Follow the Light

Although bioluminescence sometimes signals danger in the dark ocean world, it may also show where food can be found. A common source of light is **marine snow**, the organic matter that rains down constantly from the upper levels of the ocean. This material is often coated with bioluminescent bacteria that are working to break down the waste. Deep-sea animals use the bacterial glow to find and snap up delicious bits of plants, dead animals, and other nutritious debris in the snow.

An anglerfish dangles its glowing lure (inset) in front of its mouth to attract prey.

Not surprisingly, creatures that eat glowing food are strongly attracted to light and will swim toward nearly any shiny object in the hope of finding a meal. The deepwater anglerfish has developed a special way to take advantage of this behavior. An anglerfish has a flexible, antenna-like ray curving forward from its head. A pouch at the end of the ray contains bioluminescent bacteria that send a soft glow into the darkened sea. The anglerfish dangles this bluish pouch in front of its mouth and then waits for curious prey to approach. When any animal comes too close, the anglerfish opens a mouth full of needle-sharp teeth and spears its meal.

The cookie-cutter shark also uses bioluminescence as a lure. But unlike the anglerfish, which seeks smaller prey, the 3-foot (91cm)-long cookie-cutter shark goes after really big animals such as seals, dolphins, swordfish, and even whales. It attracts these animals with the help of many photophores on the underside of its body. The shark turns on its lights and swims through the water at a depth of about 600 feet (180m), where dim sunlight can still be seen. Viewed from below, most of the shark's lighted body disappears against the sunlit background. But one patch without photophores stands out clearly. Large predators think the dark patch is a little fish. They swim toward the cookie-cutter shark, thinking they are about to get an easy meal. Instead, they find that they are the meal as the shark sinks its sharp teeth into their bodies. The shark scoops out a neat ball of flesh, then zips away to eat its meal in private. The prey usually survives the attack, but it will bear a round scar for the rest of its life as the result of its cookie-cutter encounter.

The cookie-cutter shark's prey is lucky to get away with nothing worse than a painful bite. Most creatures that run into bioluminescent hunters lose their lives, not just a chunk of skin. Eating and being eaten are facts of life in the ocean world. Underwater predators hope to do plenty of eating without being eaten themselves, and bioluminescence is one of many tools that can help them do just that.

chapter

4

Staying Alive

The undersea world is a dangerous place, filled with hungry animals looking for other animals to eat. All but the very biggest sea creatures, in fact, are in danger of becoming another creature's dinner. To avoid this fate, many animals defend themselves with various forms of bioluminescence. Living lights can serve as a disguise or a distraction. They can also be used as a flashing cry for help. In some instances, bioluminescence can keep underwater predators at bay, thereby helping an animal live a long and healthy life in the ocean realm.

Shiny Camouflage

The best way to avoid being eaten is to avoid being seen in the first place. Many sea creatures use

Firefly squids confuse predators with the flickering display of their photophores.

bioluminescence as a **camouflage** to help them blend in to their surroundings. The outline of the firefly squid, for example, is hard to see because of the many photophores dotting this animal's body. Predators looking for a dark body-shaped blotch may be confused by the squid's twinkling display.

Many other sea creatures camouflage themselves with **counterillumination**, or the lighting of the lower part of the body. The light starts out as many dots from photophores. But the light spreads out as it travels through the water, so from even a short distance away, the animal seems to have a solid all-over glow. Some creatures can adjust this glow to exactly match the amount of light filtering down from

Staying Alive

above. The effect is that, from below, it is very difficult to see a counterilluminated animal against the sunlit or moonlit sea surface. A hungry predator may swim right below a tasty meal without ever realizing it is there.

Counterillumination is the main defense of the deepwater hatchetfish, which lives in all of the world's oceans. These small fish can be found as far as 12,000 feet (3.66km) below the sea surface during the daytime. At night, the hatchet fish migrate to surface regions to feed. They turn on a row of lights along their bellies to match the shifting moonlight filling the ocean waters. Between this disguise and

Feeding near the ocean surface at night, hatchetfish use lights on their bellies to camouflage themselves from predators below.

the fish's slender shape, the hatchetfish is practically impossible to spot from below.

Many other sea creatures, including most shrimp and squid species, use counterillumination to disguise themselves. One deepwater squid takes this technique a step further, changing the color of its glow automatically based on the temperature of the water. In deep water, the temperature drops, and the squid glows blue. In shallower water, the temperature rises, and the squid glows green. It does this because moonlight appears greenish near the ocean's surface but blue in deeper water. By changing its color according to the temperature, the squid always matches the surrounding light conditions.

A Glowing Distraction

Sometimes camouflage does not work, and a creature is seen and attacked by a predator. When this happens, many ocean animals use bioluminescence as a distraction. With a little luck, these animals will confuse or startle a predator so much that they can escape from danger.

The use of bioluminescent ink is one effective distraction. Some deep-sea squid and some shrimp use this technique. If threatened, these animals blast clouds of glowing liquid from their bodies, and then dart away into the darkness. Predators often attack the ink clouds instead of going after their prey. The shining ink may also blind the predator for a short

Staying Alive

A shrimp releases a cloud of glowing ink to temporarily blind and confuse a predator.

time, much as a camera's flashbulb can temporarily blind a person. With bright spots swimming in its eyes, the predator cannot see where its prey has gone. The hungry creature soon recovers its night vision—but not soon enough. By the time the predator can see clearly, the potential meal has disappeared.

Other creatures have no glowing ink but can still create brilliant displays to startle predators. One type of **hydroid**, for example, puts on an underwater fireworks show when danger approaches. Waves of light travel over and across the surface of the hydroid colony in bright sheets. Some jellyfish use a similar technique if disturbed, producing a moving series of flashes that travels around and around the edge of

Creatures That Glow

the body. Like glowing ink, these spectacular displays may temporarily blind predators. They may also scare a predator away or simply make it think twice about its intended meal. A flashing creature might be tasty, but then again, it might not. Faced with this choice, many predators will decide to look for prey that is a bit less exciting.

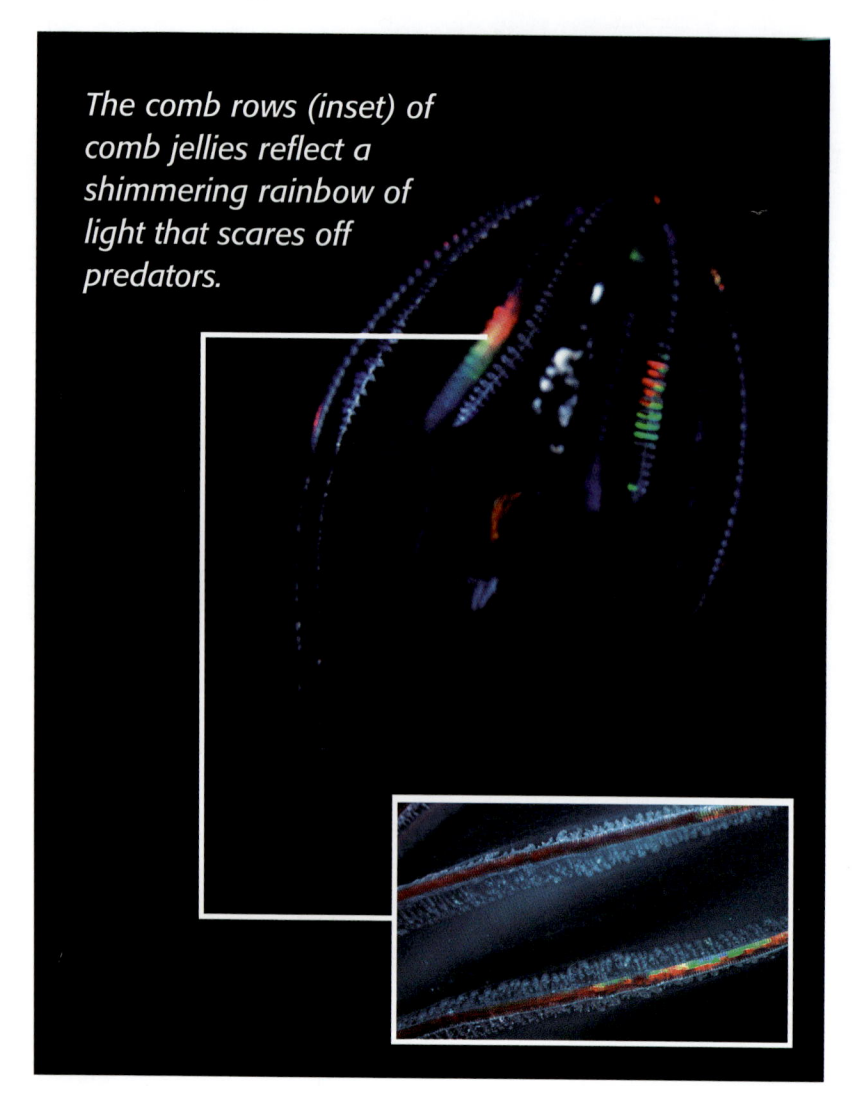

The comb rows (inset) of comb jellies reflect a shimmering rainbow of light that scares off predators.

Five-armed creatures called brittle stars use bioluminescence in an especially unusual way. If attacked, these animals make one of their arms glow bright green. Then they detach the arm from their body. The glowing arm twitches and wiggles on the ocean floor, attracting the predator's attention. While the predator is distracted, the dark body of the brittle star crawls away to safety. The brittle star will eventually grow a new arm to replace the one it dropped.

Burglar Alarm

Some small animals use bioluminescence as an alarm. When a predator comes near, these creatures flash brightly. The flash may be seen by bigger predators, which swim over to investigate. The smaller predator that triggered the flash is now in danger, so it flees. The glowing creature, on the other hand, is safe because it is too little to be noticed by the larger hunter. Scientists call this defense technique the "burglar alarm." The small predator is the burglar, and the larger predator is the cop that scares the burglar away.

Bioluminescent dinoflagellates use the burglar alarm technique to avoid being eaten. These organisms are preyed upon by tiny, shrimplike creatures called **copepods**. Even the softest touch from a copepod makes a dinoflagellate burst into light. Hungry fish and other creatures soon arrive to feed on the intruder. The copepod cannot even save itself by swimming away, since it will probably bump into many other dinoflagellates as it flees. It will give away its location by the trail of sparkles it leaves in its wake.

Deep-sea tube worms combine defenses, using both glowing ink and the burglar alarm method. These animals spit glowing ink at attackers. Because tube worms are stationary, they cannot hope to run away or distract predators for long. Instead, the glowing ink is meant to call attention to the tube worm's plight. If the tube worm is lucky, help will arrive before the predator can finish its meal.

Sometimes animals can use the burglar alarm technique even after they have been eaten. Certain small Antarctic crustaceans, for example, shine so brightly that they can be seen right through a fish's stomach. Larger predators then see and eat the shining fish, thereby removing one dangerous creature from the crustaceans' world. The original crustacean lost its life, but even after death, its glow will help keep many of its relatives safe.

The burglar alarm method and other bioluminescent defenses are clever, surprising, and often completely unexpected. They are perfect examples of how nature has equipped all its creatures, from the biggest to the smallest, with the tools they need to survive. Living lights, after all, are not just beautiful. They evolved because they are useful—and in the ocean world, nothing is more useful than staying alive.

Glossary

bacterial bioluminescence: Bioluminescence that is produced by bacteria. Many animals that cannot produce bioluminescence themselves store glowing bacteria in special sacs inside their bodies.

bioluminescence: Light that is produced by an organism through a chemical reaction.

camouflage: Body features that help an organism blend in to its surroundings.

copepods: Tiny, shrimplike creatures.

counterillumination: The lighting of the lower part of the body.

crustaceans: Hard-shelled animals with segmented bodies and antennae.

dinoflagellates: One-celled organisms. Many dinoflagellates are bioluminescent.

enzyme: A substance that starts and controls a chemical reaction.

hydroid: Soft creature related to the jellyfish and sea anemone. Hydroids usually live in colonies permanently attached to a solid surface.

infrared: Low-energy light that cannot be seen by the human eye.

intracellular bioluminescence: Bioluminescence that is produced inside a creature's cells.

luciferase: An enzyme that causes a light-producing chemical reaction.

luciferin: A protein that releases light when it reacts with oxygen.

marine snow: The organic matter that rains down constantly from the upper levels of the ocean.

organism: Any living being.

ostracods: Tiny crustaceans that use bioluminescence to attract mates.

oxyluciferin: A chemical that is produced when a luciferin combines with oxygen.

photophores: Organs that produce light through chemical reactions.

pigments: Substances that add color to other materials.

predators: Any creatures that kill and eat other creatures.

protein: A substance made by all cells. Proteins are essential for life.

receptors: Groups of cells that receive information, change it into nerve impulses, and send it to an organism's brain.

zooplankton: Microscopic floating animals.

For Further Exploration

Books

Mary Batten, *The Winking, Blinking Sea: All About Bioluminescence*. Brookfield, CT: Millbrook, 2000. This book highlights eleven underwater animals that create living light. Includes a large photo of each creature.

Sneed B. Collard, *The Deep-Sea Floor*. Watertown, MA: Charlesbridge, 2003. Travel a mile below the sea's surface to look at the geography and animal life of the ocean floor.

Edith Widder, *The Bioluminescence Coloring Book*. Fort Pierce, FL: Harbor Branch Oceanographic Institute, 1998. Developed by the world's top bioluminescence scientist, this book contains a wealth of information and pictures to color. Includes eight glow-in-the-dark paints and a paintbrush.

Web Sites

Bioluminescence Web Page (www.lifesci.ucsb.edu/~biolum). Browse through this site for all sorts of information about bioluminescence. Includes graphics and photos.

Harbor Branch Oceanographic Institution (www.biolum.org). Take an animated tour through the world of underwater bioluminescence.

Island Adventures Biobay Eco-Tours (www.biobay.com). Includes many fabulous photographs of Puerto Rico's glowing Mosquito Bay.

index

anglerfish
  bacterial bioluminescence and, 16
  hunting by, 31
  reproduction by, 23
Arabian Sea, 11

bacteria, 10
bacterial bioluminescence, 15–16
Bermuda fire worms, 23–24
bioluminescence, 6–7, 9
  chemistry of, 12, 14
  importance of, 16
  occurrence of, 7–8
  producers of, 9
  types of, 14–16
black dragonfish, 28–30
brittle stars, 39

camouflage, 33–36
cardinal fish, 27–28
chemical reactions, 12, 14
colors, 14
communication, 17–20

cookie-cutter sharks, 31–32
copepods, 39–40
counterillumination, 34–36

defenses
  burglar alarm, 39–40
  camouflage, 33–36
dinoflagellates, 10, 39–40
dwarf lantern sharks, 27

enzymes, 12, 14

firefly squids, 24, 34
fireworms, 23–24
flashlight fish
  bacterial bioluminescence and, 16
  communication by, 18–19
  hunting by, 28

habitats, 10–12, 18
hatchetfish, 23, 35–36
hunting
  illuminating prey, 28–30

45

marine snow and, 30–31
photophores patterns
and, 27–28, 31–32
hydroid colonies, 37

Indian Ocean, 11, 18
intracellular bioluminescence, 15

jellyfish, 14, 37–38

krill, 19–20

lantern fish, 23
luciferases, 12, 14, 15
luciferins, 12, 14, 15

marine snow, 30–31
milky seas, 11
Mosquito Bay (Puerto Rico), 10
mussels, 15

octopuses, 20
ostracods, 21–22

oxyluciferins, 12, 14

Pacific Ocean, 18
photophores, 15
  hunting and, 27–29, 31–32
predators, 17
proteins, 12, 14
Puerto Rico, 10

reproduction, 21–24

sharks, 27, 31–32
shrimp, 36–37
squids
  color displays of, 14, 15, 36
  defenses of, 34, 36–37
  reproduction by, 22–23, 24

tube worms, 40

worms, 23–24, 40

picture credits

Cover: © E. Widder/HBOI/Visuals Unlimited
© Harbor Branch Oceanographic Institute, 37
© Alex Kerstitch/Visuals Unlimited, 19
National Undersea Research Program/NOAA, 13, 18
Photos.com, 11 (inset), 14
© Rick Price/CORBIS, 38 (main)
© Roger Ressmeyer/CORBIS, 16
© Bruce Robinson/CORBIS, 35
© Jeffery Rotman/CORBIS, 7
Courtesy of Western Washington University, 21 (below)
© E. Widder/HBOI/Visuals Unlimited, 20, 21 (inset), 22, 26, 27, 30 (both), 34
© Douglas P. Wilson; Frank Lane Picture Agency/CORBIS, 10 (main)
© David Wrobel/Visuals Unlimited, 29, 38 (inset)

about the author

Kris Hirschmann has written more than one hundred books for children. She is the president of The Wordshop, a business that provides a variety of writing and editorial services. She holds a bachelor's degree in psychology from Dartmouth College in Hanover, New Hampshire.

Hirschmann lives just outside Orlando, Florida, with her husband, Michael, and her daughters, Nikki and Erika.